START-UP
RELIGION

GIFTS AT CHRISTMAS

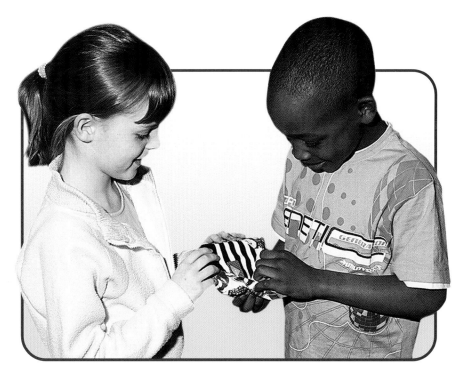

Ruth Nason

Evans

Published by Evans Brothers Limited
2A Portman Mansions
Chiltern Street
London W1U 6NR

Reprinted 2007

Produced for Evans Brothers Limited by
White-Thomson Publishing Ltd,
Bridgewater Business Centre,
210 High Street,
Lewes, East Sussex BN7 2NH

Printed in China by WKT Co. Ltd.

Consultants: Jean Mead, Senior Lecturer in Religious
Education, School of Education, University of
Hertfordshire; Dr Anne Punter, Partnership Tutor,
School of Education, University of Hertfordshire.
Designer: Carole Binding

Cover: All photographs by Chris Fairclough

British Library Cataloguing in Publication Data
Nason, Ruth
    Gifts at Christmas. - (Start-up religion)
    1. Jesus Christ - Nativity - Juvenile literature
    I. Title
    232.9'2

ISBN: 0 237 527650
13-digit ISBN 978 0 237 52765 5

Acknowledgements:
Special thanks to Sarah Crew, and to the following for
their help and involvement in the preparation of this
book: the Crew family, the Rajan family, Sharon Smith,
Wenna Taylor, the congregation of High Street Methodist
Church, Harpenden, the congregation of Upper Tooting
Methodist Church.

Picture Acknowledgements:
Carole Binding: page 7 bottom left; Mike Bramwell:
pages 21 centre and 21 bottom; The Bridgeman Art
Library: pages 14-15 (Matthias Stomer, *The Adoration
of the Magi*, Musée des Augustins, Toulouse, France);
Chris Fairclough Colour Library: pages 12, 19 top;
World Religions Photo Library: page 20.
All other photographs by Chris Fairclough.

Contents

Favourite gifts

A **gift** is a present. Think of a gift that you really liked. Why did you like it so much?

A friend brought it for me from her holiday.

My daughter painted it. It's **precious** to me.

We like new things to make.

gift   precious

cheered   favourite

Think about giving

Giving shows that you care about someone. Daniel wanted to give Natasha a present. There was a lot to think about.

What can I make that she would like?

She laughed when she dressed up as a lion. She might like a lion mask, too.

giving   care

He decided to make her a lion mask.

Which colour shall I **choose**?

Which paper shall I **wrap** it in?

What shall I write?

It fits!

choose   **wrap**   **7**

Think about receiving

► **Many people give presents at Christmas. How do you feel when you receive one?**

happy ✻ thankful ✻ excited ✻ loved ✻ special ✻

◄ **Do you try to guess what is inside?**

Christmas   receive

How can you see in the pictures that the children are pleased with their gifts?

The Christmas festival

Christmas is an important festival for Christians. It is a time when they think about the story of Jesus being born.

▶ These Christmas cards have pictures of this story on them.

Christians believe that the baby Jesus was sent by God. They believe that Jesus is God's son.

festival   Christians   Jesus   believe

Shepherd

Mary

Angel

Wise man

Shepherd boy   Jesus   Joseph

▲ These people acted the story of when Jesus was born. Can you see three wise men with gifts for Jesus?

God   shepherd   angel   wise men   11

The wise men

The wise men are part of the story that Christians remember at Christmas.

▶ These are models of them.

In the story, when Jesus was born, some wise men saw a new star in the sky. They believed it was a sign that a new king had been born. They wanted to worship him.

sign   worship

The wise men went to the city of Jerusalem, to look for the new king. Then they heard that people believed that a great king would be born one day in Bethlehem.

The wise men saw the new star again. They followed the star to Bethlehem and found Jesus there.

◄ Why do you think some people put a star on top of the Christmas tree?

Jerusalem   Bethlehem   13

The wise men's gifts

The wise men went a very long way to find Jesus.

They believed that he was a king, so they gave him three precious gifts of gold, frankincense and myrrh.

Gold was a gift for kings.

gold   frankincense   myrrh

Frankincense was burned to make sweet-smelling smoke. People believed that the smoke pleased God.

Myrrh is a perfume. When someone died, it was put on the body to show love and respect. This gift reminds Christians of the sad time when Jesus died.

perfume   love   respect

Giving love

When Christians remember the wise men, they sometimes think: "What can I give Jesus?"

They want to show Jesus that they love him. Some people say that they give Jesus their heart.

Here are some ways in which Christians say they will give their love to Jesus.

I will do what Jesus wants.

I will do my best dance for Jesus.

heart

What do you do, to show people that you love them?

pray

God's gift

Christians believe that God sent his son Jesus to tell people about God's love for everyone.

They believe that Jesus made the world a better place because he brought

love * joy * hope * peace

They say that Jesus was like a light coming to a dark world.

joy   hope   peace   candles

Often candles are used to show the idea of Jesus being like a light.

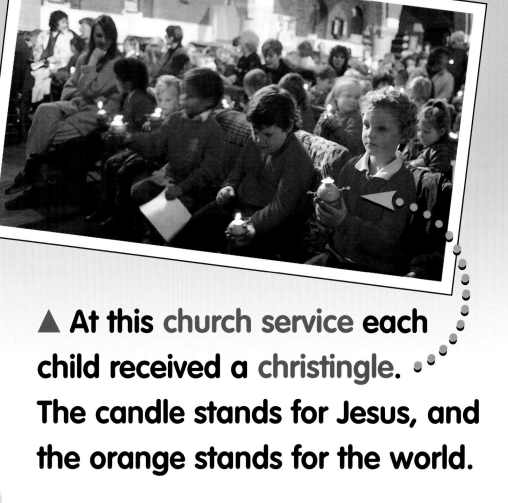

▲ At this church service each child received a christingle. The candle stands for Jesus, and the orange stands for the world.

Christians say that Jesus is the most precious gift of all. God loved people so much that he sent his son to live with them.

church   service   christingle   19

Saying thank you

Christians say thank you for God's gift of Jesus in many ways. They go to services at church to remember the story of Jesus and to praise God. They sing joyful carols.

▲ Have you heard people sing and play carols outdoors?

praise   carols

Christians want to share the joy and love they feel they have received.

▶ They give presents to each other.

◀ They also give to people in need. Children at this church gave some of their own toys, to send to poor children.

share   in need   **21**

Further information for

Background Information

■ Christmas is a cultural event, celebrated by many who are not Christians. To use it effectively for RE it is necessary to focus on the Christian festival at its core.

■ In a religiously plural school context, the belief that Jesus is God's son should not be omitted, but it should be referred to as a Christian belief.

■ Giving is a central part of the event, and can be linked to the Christian concept of Jesus as God's greatest gift.

■ The date of the birth of Jesus is unknown, and the convention of celebrating it on December 25th is totally arbitrary and did not begin until about 300 years after his birth. Therefore, use phrases like 'Christmas day is the day when Christians remember/celebrate when Jesus was born.'

■ There are two different accounts of the birth of Jesus in the Bible, Luke 2.1-20 and Matthew 2.1-12, from different sources. These are often conflated into a composite event in pictures and nativity plays, but a careful analysis of the language in Matthew shows that the wise men probably arrived at the house (not stable) in Bethlehem when Jesus was a toddler (not a baby). If possible, without arguing about the popular impression, tell the story of the wise men separately.

■ At Christmas time there are many schemes for giving to the poor that could be suitable for young children to be involved with. Christian motivation (and that of the original Santa Claus) for showing love to Jesus by giving to others can be based on Matthew 25.40.

Suggested Activities

PAGES 4-5

Discuss/show/draw children's favourite presents (but discourage one-upmanship and be sensitive if there are children who have none: perhaps ask them to show yours). Ensure understanding of gift/present vocabulary. Play a 'guess what the gift is' game with parcels of various shapes and sizes. Conduct a survey among staff (with prior prompting to elicit a range of reasons), asking what is their best-ever gift and why.

Parents and Teachers

PAGES 6-7

Let groups of children think about what gift a real child or known adult who is ill/sad/leaving would like. Make an inexpensive gift, wrap it and make a gift tag or card.

PAGES 8-9

Talk about times when it is good to give gifts, but do not make assumptions that all cultures celebrate birthdays in this way. In pairs, role-play giving and receiving gifts, and discuss how the pleasure of receiving can be shown.

PAGES 10-11

Sort a large collection of Christmas cards into sets about Jesus' birth and talk about what children know about the story. If it is Advent, sequence the cards to make a class Advent calendar or make one as a gift for younger children to use next year. Let children play with a set of 'crib' figures or dressing-up clothes and props to remind them about the story.

PAGES 12-13

Use a set of crib figures but place the wise men as far away as possible within the room and tell the story over some days, letting children gradually move the wise men nearer on their long journey. Use a star on a long stick as a prop.
Find as many stars as possible on Christmas cards, paper or decorations and use craft activities to make star decorations.

PAGES 14-15

Talk about or display popular gifts for babies. Discuss some that are for when they are older (silver spoons/Bibles).
Tell the story of Sleeping Beauty and the 'symbolic' gifts given at her birth. What would you want to give a baby? Discuss gifts that have a 'hidden' meaning, like a lead for a puppy to be collected, a pump for a bicycle or the keys of a car.
What do you think happened to the wise men's gifts?

Recommended Resources

For pages 16-17:
Give Him my Heart by Debi Gliori, Bloomsbury, 1998.

For pages 18-19:
The Children's Society provides ideas and instructions about Christingle services:

http://joshi.demonweb.co.uk/fundraise/SG_Feature/48452/12/

PAGES 16-17

Read *Give Him my Heart* by Debi Gliori, with two parallel stories about girls choosing a gift for someone important. Discuss ways of showing someone you love them, and maybe make 'gift vouchers' of a promise to do something for them.

PAGES 18-19

Make christingles with oranges, red ribbon, sticks with dolly mixture sweets and fruit, and candles (set in foil). Use the Children's Society safety guidelines and instructions (see above). Discuss what the symbols stand for.

PAGES 20-21

An effective way of tying in the inevitable 'Father Christmas' to the Christmas story is to tell the story of the 'real' Saint Nicolas/Santa Claus (if you can do so without painfully disillusioning children): he wanted to give a gift to Jesus but believed God told him to give something secretly to poor children instead.
Investigate whether a Christmas giving scheme would be appropriate for your situation.
Enjoy some carol singing.

Index